CALMING COMMUNICATION BARRIERS

Sherri Blacksher

Calming Communication Barriers

ISBN: 978 – 0 – 692 – 08547 - 9

First Edition

Published in 2018 by Get It Girl Publishing, LLC
Saginaw, MI 48601

Table of Contents

Acknowledgements

I would like to give honor, glory, and homage to my Lord and Savior Jesus Christ, whom allowed me to endure the many test and trials that I have experienced over the years, so that I may be able to share my story and encourage someone else along the way. I am truly grateful for the support my husband gave me before his demise 17 years ago. He was always excited to hear my many ideas, dreams and the desires that I had in exploring a different adventure it appeared every other year (smile) he encouraged me to dream. He was an avid reader as me. We would often talk about me writing books because of my love for writing stories, letters, and even a few plays. He would look at me in wonderment and allow me to go on and on sometimes for hours. Every now and again he would stop me and say oh Sherri you are so awesome and full of life. You just keep going on and on like the ever-ready battery! Then he would say whatever you want to do baby we can do it because I believe in you, and the only thing that makes me happy is to see you happy! Oh, my I wouldn't give to hear him say that at this point in my life.

I would like to thank my son Kuddles whom I adore with all my heart and soul, my three beautiful daughters who gave me the aspiration to go back to school because, I had to set an example for them. Kuddles is the eldest and the only male out of my four children. He had to step up to the plate after the demise of my husband and encourage my daughters to not worry me during my studies. There were so many years after the death of my husband that my son had to stay after school and over to his coach's house for practice until I got out of school because he played basketball, football, hockey, any kind of sports you can name. Many days I would pick the kids up from school after I got off at 3:00pm, they got out at 3:15 and I had to be in class @ Delta at 4:00. If my son did not have practice he would come with us. So, the kids knew the routine. We ate on the way to Delta or they ate once they got there in the Testing Learning Center. I would find a quiet safe spot for my children to get their homework done and lay down if they needed to. In between classes I would check their homework and make sure they were safe. This was not an ideal situation for them, but I could not afford daycare, and I refuse to allow anyone else to keep them. I was determined that I would get a college degree and support my children no matter what. God enabled me to become triumphant through those test and trials. So, thank you very kindly Kuddles, Jaye, Gabrielle, and Arnae for giving me a reason to live and a reason to dream!

I would like to thank my (Pooh Bear) for always having a calm quiet demeanor and knowing what to say and when to say it. Gabrielle is the one that I can talk to and she never gets excited, anxious, or on one-person side or the other☺. She has a way without saying much bring homeostasis in our family. She is on all our side and she loves us all very much! Thank you Pooh for your kind spirit and always telling me that I am smart and can't anybody stop me from doing what I want to do.

I would like to thank my oldest daughter Jaye, who looks just like me but does not act like me. I feel like I owe a quarter of my 4 degrees to her. Many nights I woke her up from her sleep in a panic state "Jaye I just lost my 10-page paper!" She would get up out of a sound sleep and retype if she could not recover my papers over the last 13 years☺ I can never repay her for those countless hours of sleep she lost because of me. I am a writer by nature, she would look at the rubric and say, "mom this paper should be 3 pages and it is 10 we are going to shorten it" and I would say NO! Needless, to say she would redo it. I love you

Jaye from the bottom of my heart and if it was not for you allowing me to express my thoughts on paper 3 times the requirement, I would not be the writer I am today!

To Arnae, the last of the Mohegans, I would like to thank you for being the mother hen of us all☺ This young person has been an anchor in my life by encouraging and pushing me to be all that I can be. I thank you Arnae for believing in me as a Mother, Pastor, Scholar, Entrepreneur, and as a person. You have been that person that told me so what if you failed, get back up and try it again. Thank you for pushing and reminding me that failure is never an option! Because of my babies I rise to the call of "I am who I say that I am" and no one else has that right!

My mom, who I can truly say is the strongest human being that I have encountered on this earth, has been such an inspiration to me as she has had many, many battles to conquer herself such as, over- coming blindness, 20 something aneurisms on the brain, beating cancer 4 times, recovering from a stroke, along with some horrible tragedies as a young person. She has taught me what true resilient mean. It is because of God and my mother that I believe that I am unstoppable in reaching my goals. Watching her conquer her trials alone have convinced me that the race is not given to the swiftest, but to the one that endures to the ends. So, I can say Yes! Mom though you were being tested you continue to stress to me that I can do all things through Christ which strengthens me!!! So, words cannot express how much you have inspired, encouraged, and empowered me to keep on pushing forward and to never give up on my dreams. My mom even wrote a paper about me titled "The Women with Many Facets in Life" several years ago in college and got an A on the paper!

To my sisters, Sharon & Tonja Hopkins. Sharon, I can't thank her enough. She has been an inspiration to me none stop for 50ish years.

Sharon, I thank you from the bottom of my heart for always being there from the time we were kids, we have been inseparably close. We have shared so many good, bad and indifferent times together. Thanking Sharon would take an entire book in its entirety. Sharon has been my sister, mentor, counselor, adviser, friend, greatest supporter, biggest critic, my ride a die, partner in good crimes, motivator, cheer leader, and the person that believed in me when literally no one believed in me! We experienced so much in life together. This is the person in my life that knows everything about me. We slept in the same bed, wore the same clothes, smoked cigarettes together, partied together, and were pregnant at the same time as roommates, ministry and the celebration of over twenty years of sobriety together. It seems like a life time ago that we use to party! LOL!!! Thank God. He knew that we did not know what we were doing so He intervened and said, "I have other plans for you two"! Well needless to say if it was no Sharon this Sherri that's writing this book would probably not exist! Through it all my sister has remained a constant solid rock in my corner, never saying no to me even when she should have. Sharon, I am proud to call you my sister and my friend! Thanks for all you have done and all that I am going to continue to need you to do! (Smile)!

Tonja Michelle Hopkins, my youngest sister the spoil but brat out of the family. Thanks for all your encouraging words, the special support that you gave me when my husband died. You came and helped me got everything sorted out at a time when I did not know if I was going or coming. Thank you for your encouraging words to my children when they needed it most and I was so torn until I didn't know what to say even though I was trying. Thank you for encouraging me in my ministry and thank you for driving the highway and by ways many of times from Tennessee to Michigan to see about your family! I love and appreciate all you have done and as my sister, and I want you to know that I will continue to need you as a part of my life. My only brother Bernard I thank you for believing in whatever I say! Whenever I tell my brother about something I want to do or try he always say "Oh …. Sherri, you can do it!!! I thank you for never doubting me and encouraging me to do whatever it is I want to do! My brother is just laid back and too cool!

I have a very special friend that I would love to thank that helped encouraged me to start back writing and to become the person that I am today. His mild mannerism of assuring me that it does not make sense for me to settle for less empowered me with the strength to persevere through some of my saddest hours. I thank God that because of him I had the amazing chance to learn how to love again when I never thought I would!

I would also like to thank my absolute favorite, faithful, loving, caring, and encouraging cousin/sister Mrs. Effie Bee Allen! I thank you for being that sounding block that I could share anything with at any time of day or night. I thank you for encouraging me when I needed it, patting my back and telling me it's going to be alright when I did not believe it was going to be! I thank you for allowing me to cry on your shoulders and for sharing countless stories with you over the years☺ I thank you for loving me unconditionally my cousin no matter what!

Last but certainly not least, my awesome Publisher: Dr. Laura Brown who spent hours of going backward and forward with me until I was totally satisfied with this Masterpiece! This has been a journey that came along with many doubts and uncertainties, but we continue to persevere despite me wanting to give up and Dr. Brown would not allow me. She remained calm and unmoved when I was hysterical☺ Bless her heart! Dr. Laura Brown, I can say if there were no you at this point in my life there would be no

CALMING COMMUNICATION BARRIERS!!!

I commend you for your steadfast work with this collaborative project of ours!

AGAIN, I SAY THANK YOU

Preface
What Creates Communication Gaps?

Steven R. Covey, the author of the favorite 7 Habits of Highly Successful People, suggests that a person "seek first to understand, then to be understood." In every segment of life whether professional or personal, communication gaps wreak havoc on relationships, resulting in hurt feelings, broken alliances, lost profits and more. Reasons and theories abound about what causes a communication gap are many, and the explanations are as diverse as they are plentiful. Although the answers for the cause of the difference are varied, it is clear to all that the necessity of a bridge is irrefutable. Not only is the existence of the gap undeniable, but it is also indiscriminative in its reach. Which means it touches people from the boardroom to the bedroom, from the courthouse to the church house, from educators to elected officials, from parents to professionals, miscommunication rears its divisive head at every level and in every place. And yet, everyone wants to be understood, to have their message received as intended free from misconstrued meaning or intent.

Although the communication gap arises for assorted reasons, there are consistent benchmarks that are worth exploring. First, **Mistrust** is a lack of trust, and suspicion. There are times when one or more persons is apprehensive about another's motives and intentions thus causing a wariness about the truthfulness of their conversation. The one element that creates a healthy relationship is **trust**; consequently, when there is an element of suspicion or lack of confidence, the connection is tepid at best and contentious at its worst. Distrust frequently stems from a selfish or a "me first" attitude that leads to conflict, competition, contention. In professional environments mistrust is rampant as employees' jockey for position and status, knowing that individuals with the most influential jobs are likely to have high status. Unfortunately, this type of a competitive environment sometimes leads to chaos and gaps in communication. The differences occur because individuals do not feel safe sharing information that might potentially hinder their forward motion within the organization. Safety is vital to transparency in communication; one requires reassurances that their vulnerability will not be used against them or exposed without their expressed consent.

Human emotions are fragile at times even in the most reliable person; therefore, people tend to guard them with fierce intensity. When one feels safe, they freely explore their surroundings and are open in their discussion. There is a sense of security that allows freedom in the communication flow. It's like having a partner that you trust based on time spent and experiences shared, you have more favorable outcomes than negatives, so you built trust over time.

Secondly, there is the **miscommunication** or communication that was either conveyed wrong or received wrong. Whenever miscommunication is present in a relationship, the atmosphere for open and mutual sharing is non-existence. Rather than transparent communication where everybody's point of view and opinions enjoy the freedom of expression, the discussion suffers. Often it is difficult to get to the heart of a matter in a brief time frame when people think hidden agendas are present. Open communication is a necessity. When those involved in a conflict of communication they often refuse to speak up because they don't want to offend others. There is always that possibility that sharing their perceived understanding will result in adverse consequences toward them. Consequently, the problem-solving process becomes a treasure hunt. People want to think that they are safe to share

Openly about problems and workable solutions. You see; communication sounds fundamental, however, don't believe for a moment that everyone has the same understanding of a shared conversation. There is an old story of a man in communication with a friend as he sits back rubbing his stomach after eating a great meal and says: "I have eaten sufficient," his friend replies, "say you went fishing?", the man reiterates, "I have eaten plenty," his friend replies, "say you caught twenty?", exasperated the man shakes his head saying, "poor soul," to which the friend replies, "Say you broke your pole?" Words and conversations are easily miscommunicated and misunderstood. Calming Communication Barriers seeks to expose the basis of miscommunication and offer solutions to closing the communication gap in that area.

Thirdly, a communication gap arises because of **Ineffective Communication.** Many people erroneously think communication is as comfortable as opening your mouth and speaking. Quite the contrary, how many times are words and conversations misunderstood merely because the speaker did not adequately convey their message? Some of the "common sense' things we think about communication are wrong. Some discussion "facts" are myths and misconceptions; therefore, Calming Communication Barriers will strive to tear down the myths while unveiling the truth about effective communication. Ineffective communication is a leading cause of a breakdown in the communication process. There are times when the sender of a message is unclear with their messaging, and the receiver is unsure how to respond, and subsequently, neither person is satisfied with the outcome.

Fortunately, there are indicators, which are markers or measurements illustrating an ineffective communicator that I will explore in detail in a subsequent chapter of this book. Here are a few examples; interrupting, indirectness, through hints, lack of conciseness, complaining, close-mindedness, a lack of enthusiasm and confidence. We will look at these indicators closely and encourage you to judge your scale of effectiveness prior to expressing yourself.

Fourthly, A **Lack of Communication** is another cause of a communication gap. Whereas poor communication is frustrating in the workplace and other relationships, a lack of communication is equally disappointing and damaging. Just as one can over communicate, a shortage of discussion opens the door for others to try to fill in the gaps without the needed information to correctly convey a message or perform a task. Often, it is difficult to get to the bottom of a matter in a timely fashion when people don't speak up. The most efficient way to solve a communication problem is to speak up! If you don't want others to make assumptions about what you want or what you mean, make sure you don't hold back exactly how you feel. Communication is a necessity, and effective communication transpires when a leader can facilitate an open dialogue between people who trust their intentions.

Lastly, the communication gap that I will address in this book is **No Communication.** At first glance, this seems redundant, after all, we just talked about lack of communication, but no transmission is the absence of discussion altogether or a wall of silence. Contrary to the famous quote, silence is not always golden; it can be deadly. Where there is no communication, there is no direction, and people fail without proper guidance and direction. Without adequate disclosure, many assumptions are made that could prove detrimental to an organization or a relationship.

Since the communication problem is a people problem, then it is necessary also to understand the personalities of individuals. Calming communication Barriers will delve into three types of people who influence a company, a group, or a personal relationship either positively or negatively. **Loafers, Leeches, and Lifters** are personalities that one will encounter in any environment. George Bernard Shaw wrote, "The greatest problem with communication is the illusion that it has been accomplished" (Shaw, 2011). People often think they have communicated clearly and yet their message is often confusing to others.

Calming Communication Barriers

Notes

Prologue

C alming Communication Barriers- is a book that is close to my heart for several reasons. I have found over the years that I have been misunderstood on numerous occasions or the intents of my message was misconstrued for one reason or another. Communication is an area that we all can improve in. Communication is the essence of life. Daily millions of messages are sent and received both nonverbal and verbal.

Whether it's someone making a speech, a billboard promoting a product, or someone communicating with each other. Communication has the power to change and shape society, cultures, and individual lives.

I am a true advocate for effective communication. I look around in my own life and realize how ineffective communication has affected me by causing me to resign from a job, walk away from organizations I loved, walk around my house not communicating with family members, and significant others for days, and placing unnecessary strains on other relationships only to later find out it was simply a misunderstanding due to a lack of communication. When I shared with others on the topic of my book, they all said it is a Win- Win topic that needs to be dealt with.

So, like always I consulted with the head of my life whom I choose to call "God" and He said to me focus on simple everyday strategies that we need to apply to our conversations with purpose. By taking a step back so to speak, put ourselves in the receiver's shoes and then speak. Now we are speaking with great intentions, because we are having reservations prior to speaking.

IT IS WITH MY SINCERE REGARDS THAT YOU FIND THESE

CALMING COMMUNICATION STRATERGIES AND TOOLS EMPOWERING, IN HELPING YOU TO OVERCOME COMMUNICATION BARRIERS IN THE FUTURE!!!

Chapter 1
Mistrust

M istrust is the lack of trust or to have the confident expectation that someone's motives and intentions are less than noble. In other words, you don't trust the individual to have your best interest at heart or to have the same right intent towards you. Where there is an absence of trust, vulnerability and transparency are impossible. People need to feel safe sharing intimate information. Many times, people are comfortable sharing their strengths, but they tightly guard their weaknesses. Trust is the core of a functioning, cohesive organization, team, or relationship. In the context of organizational communication, trust is the confidence that your coworker's intentions are pure and that there is no reason to guard your ideas or opinions for fear of ridicule, retribution, or retaliation. Sometimes the mistrust stems from a lack of experience with a new group or an unpleasant experience with the group; never the less, people will never reach their full potential with mistrust at its core. When you have previous experience that a specific person delivers quality work consistently, you trust that they will do it again.

To have a solid foundation of trust requires team members to act bravely and make themselves vulnerable to each other. Achieving confidence based on an elevated level of vulnerability does not come naturally because many people in the workplace are highly competitive. It is not natural to openly disclose you are deficient in any specific skill set. Quite the opposite, people usually work hard to conceal any skill deficits they might have. However, this type of behavior is counter-productive to achieving the success an individual or organization desires. Unfortunately, teams, organizations, groups, individuals who refuse to become vulnerable, end up spending significant amounts of time managing their behaviors and masking their true selves because of fear and mistrust.

Subsequently, it is next to impossible for a new company to win the trust of a new employee soon after they join the staff. Through no fault of their own, the new employee brings with them the mistrust they suffered at their former place of employment. Transparent communication is the remedy for distrust. Transparency, where everyone involved point of views and concerns are freely expressed. Often it is difficult to get to the bottom of a matter promptly when people don't speak up. Communication is a necessity. That's why those involved in a conflict tends not to speak up, fearing job loss, exposing others, or their wrongdoings.

At this point, the problem-solving process becomes a treasure hunt, and the quest is trust. Since communication is a two-way process, when the process suffocates due to mistrust and a lack of the flow of information or dialogue between two or more persons, it is inevitable that problems will arise. Questions left to sort themselves will never be solved, when in fact the answer is as simple as gaining an understanding of the other party's expectations. The unmasking process is sometimes painful as well, because individuals present a persona of their choosing whether it is factual or manufactured. Never the less, it is the uninterrupted flow of communication that paves the way to building genuine trust leading to the successful completion of projects, collaborations and healthy relationships. Just like a highly collaborative and communicative workplace promotes employee productivity, inspiration, and creativity, the same is true for personal associations, and other organizations.

Unfortunately, many people feel uncomfortable asking for clarity about shared communication, tasks, and goals, although sharing tends to boost one's self confidence along with the ability to communicate effectively. The leader or leaders of an organization shoulder the responsibility to ensure their workplace has an atmosphere conducive to the free flow of information sharing without the fear of retribution or open rebuke. Teams that conceal pertinent information when communicating limit their potential for exponential growth and success.

Where there is an environment of trust, people don't hesitate to ask for help, give help, and receive constructive feedback. When the workplace, church house, or home is deemed safe by members, individuals don't jump to conclusions about others in their company. Mistrust causes one to assume the worst even while secretly hoping for the best. It also deprives the entire team of the full benefit of everyone's talents and skills. Mistrust places a barrier between the diverse members of the same workplace, church, and in your personal life. Because you want the best possible outcome for your business, organization, church, and personal relationship, it is necessary to do the intentional work to overcome the experiences of the past to move forward.

How does one turn the tide of mistrust into trusting again? It is not a simple feat, but if you are willing, let us look at some steps to point you in the right direction.

Calming Mistrust Barriers

1. Be open about your weaknesses. Don't be afraid to ask for help, it shows your willingness to learn, and respect for your teammates, co-workers, peers, Pastor, fellow members, family, and friends.
2. Show respect for other areas of responsibility, ask them about their duties. Be open to learning something that is not in your area of responsibility.
3. Offer constructive feedback and help.
4. Do not focus on trivial matters such as gossip, innuendo, unfounded criticism or other destructive behaviors.
5. Be quick to apologize.
6. Learn conflict resolution strategies or bring in an experienced facilitator.
7. Be Observant. Is there tension in the air? Address it immediately.
8. Don't seek to blame, seek solutions.
9. Identify any current trust problems and address them.
10. Transparency is crucial.

Of course, there are other steps or suggestions, but start with these, and you will be well on your way to rebuilding trust.

If you are a leader, you must lead the way by example. You must not allow the misdeeds of the past to cloud your leadership ability today and into the future. Be the first to demonstrate the vulnerability, to admit your mistakes and short-comings. Make sure you create an environment that is judgment free and is not a place of fear. Remember, as the leader those who follow will mimic your behaviors.

Calming Strategies

1. **Lunch and Learn**. Take a person to lunch that you don't know. Perhaps choose someone of a different race, a superior or subordinate, a different generation, or a different faith. Make sure you seek to understand, lay aside assumptions, and remain open-minded.

2. **Lean In.** Make sure you follow up with your new acquaintances. After lunch and learn, have a follow-up conversation to make sure the person knows you heard and understood them. Remind them of something specific they talked about, so they know you are genuine.

3. **Admit Your Mistakes.** Be quick to admit if you have made a mistake, it shows your willingness to be open. Don't be the know it all in the workplace, home, church, or other personal relationships.

4. **Ask Questions** and WAIT for the answers.

5. **Let's Make a Deal.** Collaborate on a project with someone and make sure you over deliver on your part.

6. **Come In**. Maintain an open- door policy, free of judgment and retribution.

7. **Observe and Serve.** Notice when individuals or groups show signs of tension and address it quickly and effectively.

8. **Sincerity Shines.** Authenticity breeds trust.

9. **Show Up in the Room.** Be where you need to be.

10. **Honesty is the Best Policy.** Don't sacrifice the truth for your ego.

Keep a journal and record what you learn and if any of the strategies helped to calm the communication gap refer back to them.

Notes

Chapter 2
Miscommunication

M iscommunication is to communicate mistakenly, unclearly, or inadequately. Miscommunication is quickly rectified by asking clarifying questions, although the answer is simple in practice, human behavior makes it difficult. Employees and others must feel comfortable asking for clarification, which can boost the employee's confidence and ability to communicate effectively. A highly collaborative and communitive environment promotes employee's productivity, inspiration, and creativity. When an employee does not understand their assigned task, it causes confusion and possible low-self -esteem.

Unfortunately, miscommunication happens often, but it is avoidable when one is vigilant about polishing their conversations and deliveries. At times, people are lazy with their discussions, assumptions, bare assertions, and misunderstandings occur. It is essential to take caution in every conversation because the possibility to harm is present. For example, when an employer is transmitting information in written form, they should try to think of the reader and keep directions simple, specific, and to the point, leaving no room for error. Also, Leaders need to make sure the reader feels comfortable enough to ask questions if the directions are unclear.

One of the most important habits you can adopt is to check in with the person with whom you are engaged in conversation with to make sure yours and their understandings are equal. Always remember to think before you speak. In our haste to get our point across, we inadvertently blurt out the wrong things sometimes. Don't be in such a rush to get the information out that you fail to check and double check your message to make sure it is clear, concise, and is understood by the receiver. Give yourself ample time to organize your thoughts and words. Consider writing some notes for yourself to make sure you stay focused.

Additionally, keep in mind that one must be resilient in their obligations to sustain and create harmony with others. Therefore, be mindful of your attitude and tone when communicating. Most times it's not what you say, but it is how you say it. A poor view will reproduce poor attitudes in others. The receiver in a conversation will often mimic the tone of the sender. When speaking, make sure your sound matches the content of the conversation, it is never okay to become explosive. If you exercise empathy and think of the receiver more than you need to be right, you will likely communicate adequately. Remember you don't want just to talk, but instead, you seek to understand first and the be understood secondly.

Although we don't think about it, often semantics are another source of miscommunication. Your word choice and how we use the words, along with their meaning could cause miscommunication errors. The same words used by a leader and a subordinate can have an entirely different sense to each of them. For example, technical experts create specialized terminology that only someone in their occupational field has a working knowledge of the language. Culture also impacts the communication process. Different ethnicities have their unique style of conversing that makes it difficult for an outsider to comprehend. So, for clarity's sake, don't use culturally intimate terms with those who don't have that same connection.

Remember, gaining the attention of the one you want to engage is critical. It is easy for misunderstandings to occur when one of the participants in the communication process is inattentive or distracted. Make sure the person understands your words, be careful to ensure a language barrier does not exist. In today's multicultural society it is highly likely to have a communication with someone whose dominant language is different than yours. Be careful not to offend with inappropriate body language, word choice, or tone.

When attempting to gain the other person's attention, make sure you are not an interloper while they are in the middle of something. Even if you are the leader, manager, supervisor, or spouse, it is imperative to show the other person that you respect what they are doing but make it understandable that you need to communicate with them.

Another way to tamp down miscommunication is not to assume. The different perception of others is a significant reason why leaders need to communicate effectively. Emotionally it is hard and can be crippling to trust others. An assumption based on outward perception is rarely right as there are too many variables that are not evident. For instance in the workplace physical conditions are often masked by employees because they fear if noticed they may have to go home and miss a day's wages. Therefore, if you see someone with a sour look on their face, don't assume they have a terrible attitude, it could be a physical condition or several other benign reasons.

It is important to know that assumption also blocks accurate communication, because of assumed reasons a judgment is made without the benefit of asking the person. Consequently, you miss out on the opportunity to get to know the person beyond the superficial niceties. Assuming breeds miscommunication and it is taking the lazy way out of communicating with someone. Let's face it, useful communication takes work, and many refuse to put forth the effort.

After assuming, a lack of courtesy is high on the list of reasons for miscommunication. There was a time when we were called a polite society, well, that is not true today. Because we are such a rushed and stressed society, politeness has fallen by the wayside and is replaced by expediency. A work environment that has an atmosphere of rudeness and sarcasm is a highly stressful and undesirable workplace. It is the type of place where you are reluctant to arrive and are in a hurry to leave! The irony is not readily understood by everyone and is easily perceived as rudeness. Be courteous and leave your sarcasm at the door.

With all the many ways miscommunication occurs a leader who has honed their human skills can alleviate many of the problems. Human skills are primarily concerned with working with people, which is demonstrated in the way that one perceives a superior, equal, and subordinates per subsequent behavior. An individual with highly developed human skills is aware of the beliefs of other people, assumptions, and their attitude. They can accept other viewpoints and opinions that are different from one's own. They are also skilled in understanding and is a good judge of character about what other people mean by their words and behavior.

In today's global society and workforce, human skills are vital for enduring success. One cannot treat everyone like they are the same culturally; being insensitive to difference can cause the death of a relationship and kill productivity and growth. In some cultures, speaking loudly is the norm, while in another ethnicity speaking loudly is considered rude. In the United States, we teach our employees, those seeking jobs, our youth, and others, to look the person you are engaging in the eyes. We view direct eye contact as a sign of respect and showing attentiveness. But, in another cultural context, direct eye contact is considered rude and disrespectful. Be mindful and educate yourself on the communication customs of the people with whom you work, worship, dating, or doing business with. Below are some things to help.

Calming Miscommunication Barriers

1. Consider who you are engaging. Is there a cultural difference? Do you speak the same language? Keep your words simple.
2. Remember communication is transactional: the conversation is meant to go back and forth. Don't hog the conversation. Always make sure your message is understood.
3. Engage actively and listen with your eyes and ears.
4. Try to reach a mutual understanding through additional dialogue beyond the initial conversation.
5. Don't speak before you complete your thought process. Plato said wise men talk because they have something to say, while fools speak because they must say something. Think it through before you speak.
6. Overcome inattentiveness. Pay attention to the conversational process. Listen, Listen, Listen!
7. Retain what you hear. Don't quickly forget what a speaker is saying, hold it tight in your memory.
8. Control the amount of information you share. Sometimes information overload occurs, be careful not to share too much at one time.
9. Be mindful of misunderstandings. Repeat and clarify for mutual understanding. Look for any confusion.
10. Misinterpretation. Make sure the message is correctly interpreted. Be aware of any language or cultural differences.

Calming Miscommunication Strategies

1. Educate yourself about the diverse cultures within your organization. Get to know someone who is ethnically different and allow them to teach you their communication style.

2. Create cultural awareness days within your organization. Allow time for employees to showcase their various cultures and fully participate. On these days have a panel of "experts" (fellow employees) available to answer questions either in a public forum or privately.

3. Hold interactive communication workshops in the workplace. Arrange mock scenarios that highlight common miscommunication problems and address them in creative but useful ways.

4. Establish email protocols and guidelines that are easy to understand and practice. Write a co-worker or supervisor and have them critique the clarity and appropriateness of your message. Pay attention to their feedback and make the necessary adjustments.

5. Practice clarity and conciseness. Practice in front of a mirror, look at your facial expressions and your stance. Are you welcoming or not? Also, record yourself and make any needed changes to your vocal tone and quality.

6. Learn your non-verbal cues. Are you sending the wrong messages unintendedly?

7. Keep your conversation simple. Do not try to impress with your expansive vocabulary. It is best to be understood rather than impressive but confusing.

8. Keep your distance. Don't over-step the physical communication boundaries. Make sure you honor immediacy, don't become too familiar. Pay attention to what seems comfortable or uncomfortable for the other person.

9. Be the Problem-solver. Clear up confusion quickly and efficiently.

10. Learn to speak clearly and completely. Refuse "lazy speech", slang that is culture specific.

Notes

Chapter 3
Ineffective Communication

Ineffective communication occurs when we place our communication process on autopilot, and we neglect to monitor how we both send and receive information. Ineffective communication can create problems that create both long-term and short-term issues; for example, when multiple staff or departments in an organization work different shifts there is a staff variation of reporting times, this can interfere with consistent sharing of information. Information is at times not efficiently transferred or is missed altogether, possibly resulting in low employee motivation and morale.

People need to have confidence in their oneness and have it nurtured through the clarity and consistency of shared information. Confidence is imperative to the openness of individuals to share information freely. At times it is necessary for team members or individuals in diverse relationships to share sensitive information, these disclosures require an elevated level of vulnerability and those involved need assurance their communication receives proper handling. Improper handling of information includes misunderstanding the meaning of the message, gossiping about information shared, taking concerns of an individual lightly, and creating an environment of fear.

An active leader's goal is to minimize problems and to meet them head-on before situations escalate and become uncontrollable. Indeed, leaders need resiliency in their obligations to create and sustain a harmonious environment for their organization. Leaders should be keenly aware of those who sabotage effective communication by delving into power-plays, self-promotion, ploys, and corporate politicking. Employees at times engage in unhealthy competition with the intent to destroy the perceived competition.

While a competitive environment can spur healthy growth and improvement, workplace competition can put workers against each other when they and the company are better off working together. High stress and defensiveness are telltale signs of an overly competitive work environment when competition becomes the zero-sum game; it is evident that the competitive environment is no longer constructive but is destructive. A healthy competitive environment allows all workers to perform at their highest levels while encouraging others to do the same. The end goal is that the competitive climate helps positive individual achievement while ensuring continued growth, innovation, and profitability of the entire organization.

Ineffective communication can have a detrimental effect on any organization, whether it is professional, religious, and civilian. There is a well- defined correlation between ineffective communication and adverse outcomes in the entities success or failure. If it is true that adequate communication builds trust, loyalty, and healthy relationship with others, then it is safe to conclude that ineffective communication destroys trust, reliability, and erodes relationships. Therefore, it is mandatory to work to master the communication process.

Since communication is a two-way process of reaching mutual understanding, in which participants not only exchange information, news, ideas, and feelings but also create and share meaning. In general, communication is a means of connecting people and places; ineffective communication inhibits the process of joining people through exchanging of information and more. There are many types of barriers that can cause weak interface, and the results are unfavorable to the success of an organization if it is not corrected. Leaders must focus on how important it is to be able to communicate both internally and externally in a company. Miscommunication readily occurs where ineffective communication presents. Persons receiving information from their superiors should let it be known that some miscommunication happened when uncertainty results during communication.

There are times when the success of a project is thwarted because of an ineffective interface, where the participants weren't on the same page because the expectations were not synched. At this point, an investigation needs to happen to pinpoint the cause of the breakdown. Every one of the communication processes requires a thorough examination as to their viability. Some changes might occur, but that's okay, no matter how small the difference is, change in the right direction usually warrants the positive change.

Communication inefficiencies create extreme environments; low morale, affects productivity and time wasted trying to establish clarity thereby causing monetary loss, job turnover, job safety cost, and corporate changes. One should never assume communication is effective without checking with the recipient. Since the connection is a complex activity that involves voice tone, volume, body language, prejudgment of the topic, and the communication history of the participants. Also, the personality of the sender and the receiver impacts the effectiveness of communication as well. Personality is recognized as a concept of predicting a person's work ethic. An individual's personality helps determine how a person responds and processes environmental features and situational cues at work and other environments. Some personalities are bright, and some are dark, and both have a direct effect on our conversational styles.

People with bright personality traits are optimistic, and they view life through optimistic lens. Therefore, their communication is usually upbeat, light, encouraging, and agreeable. They are confident people and are more likely to be capable communicators because they seek to understand others and they are open-minded. Whereas those with dark personality traits such as narcissism, Machiavellian, and psychopathic they tend to be lean more towards ineffective communication.

Ineffective communicators focus on self and are not interested in understanding the message of another person or do they care if their words are understood; their focus is to be heard. The problem arises when a leader has dark personality traits, and the organization they lead is affected negatively. Dark personality traits drive employees, collaborators, and customers away. Fight, flight, and freeze is the consequences of ineffective communication. Incompetent leadership and managerial behaviors in an organization cause havoc among the employees, leaving them confused and insecure about their work status.

There is an array of barriers that lead to ineffective communication, below are a few, but there are many.

Barriers of Effective Communication

1. **Noise.** It seems obvious, but how often have you engaged in conversation amid loud noises such as music, competing discourses, full auditorium, classrooms, churches, any busy workplace. Imagine a supervisor walking the floor of a noisy machine shop stopping to speak with an employee. Do you think the message received is the exact message conveyed? Probably not!

2. **Messy thoughts.** Sometimes people speak before they take the time to organize their thoughts. Consequently, the communication is confusing and hard to follow. Have you ever asked someone if they were following you, and they said no? Perhaps your message was too messy and hard to follow because of gaps and stray thoughts. Tidy up your thoughts before you speak!

3. **Audience Ignorance**. Have you ever listened to a speaker and you left disappointed because their message did not capture you, because it did not relate to who you are? It is difficult to communicate with someone you don't know; you must educate yourself on the background and culture, of your audience. If you take the time to know your audience, you can send a compelling message that is well received and understood.

4. **Tone and Pitch.** Make sure you are aware of your tone and the pitch. Different audiences require different tones and pitch that are acceptable to the receiver. What is fair to one

person maybe offensive to another, again, know your audience.

5. **Verify.** With the receiver that they understand your intended message. Sometimes people will nod their head as though they understood the message when they really didn't. Verification is critical; take the time to do it!

6. **Understand different viewpoints, and respect varying opinions.** Understand that more than one opinion can co-exist, the world is big enough to accommodate another perspective; are you?

7. **Unreasonable Expectations others.** Don't expect others to think, act, or speak just like you.

8. **Attitudinal Barriers.** There are many personality types within one group or organization. Learn to navigate the multidimensional personality types.

9. **Emotional Intelligence.** Developing your emotional intelligence will help you manage your stress and the stress of others and form successful interpersonal relationships.

10. **Self-Awareness.** Have conscious knowledge of your own character, feelings, motives and desires.

Calming Ineffective Communication Strategies

1. Be clear, concise, and consistent. Don't over communicate, keep it simple, get to the point. Stay on message, so the listener doesn't have to work hard to decipher the intent, make it understandable!

2. Don't try to impress, communicate to have an understanding and reach a consensus.

3. Turn down all competing noises. If you are in a noisy area, move to a quieter area. Let your listener know that it is crucial that they hear and understand your message.

4. Gather your thoughts before you talk! Stay away from sputtering, give yourself time to organize your message. Garbled thoughts equal a confused message and receiver!

5. Put your receiver at ease, do your homework. before you speak know who you are talking to or with. If you are speaking to an audience of more than one, remember the common background and the goal of the gathering. If you are talking to one person, make them feel special because you did due diligence and you know how to speak on their level of understanding.

6. Empathize. Wear the shoes of those who need the information to fulfill their roles. Understand that it's not about you, it's about reaching the intended goal. Do not allow ineffective communication to derail the entire goal.

7. Take full responsibility for your response or lack thereof. Understand that no matter the circumstances you alone are

responsible for the quality of your communication, you have the responsibility to be effective in your communication.

8. Clarify, Clarify, And Clarify! Makes sure those with whom you are communicating with are crystal clear about your message and its intent.

9. Specify! Don't leave it up to the listener to fill in the gaps; they might get it wrong, working with false assumptions.

10. Stinginess clogs the communication pipeline. Make sure you share enough to keep the communication process flowing smoothly and freely.

Notes

Chapter 4
Lack of Communication in Your Professional & Personal Life

A lthough it is imperative to talk about the barriers to effective communication, what happens when you are faced with the unmovable obstacle of silence or a lack of communication? Communication is a two-way process between two or more participants, but what happens when the other individual decides not to cooperate Or, what about a flawed communication process that causes chaos? A cohesive organization must have an efficient, uninterrupted process that routinely allows messages to flow from one area to another. A strong leader recognizes the importance of consistent communication throughout the company. Where there is a lack of communication, individuals will try to fill the vacuum with miscommunication, rumors, gossip, and ambiguity.

Subordinates look to their supervisors and managers to share pertinent information to help them achieve their position objectives; they also expect an open- door policy that allows them to walk through the door and share their concerns and get answers to all their questions. They assume they will receive a sympathetic ear and sincere empathy. They would like to believe that they are an integral part of the information pipeline, and they should reasonably expect an open channel of communication.

Climate control is one of the fundamental functions a head supervisor should possess as a leader in ministry, head of a household, an administrator in healthcare, or an educational institution. They are the ones to determine the scope and amount of information that is disperse throughout an organization. An atmosphere that allows the free flow of information, ideas, and business goals, stimulates growth and productivity for the business and their staff.

In business, communication must continue long after a new hire takes the company tour and receives the company history, goals, and expectations. Imagine a healthcare system where there is a change in medical personnel at the end of a shift and none of the previous personnel shares the medical information and significant patient information they encountered throughout the day. The results could possibly be life-threatening. Likewise, religious institutions withholding information about a leader or Sunday school worker with an unethical background could put vulnerable Christians at risk.

The two essential functions that communication serves in an organization are disseminating the information needed by employees to get things done and to build commitment and trust. Without trust and commitment staff works without clear directions, they have shallow goals and minimal opportunity for advancement.

The negative impact of lack of communication affects everyone, people began to feel disenfranchised and disheartened that they're a part of the organization where they don't feel significant; instead, they start to feel dehumanized. Consequently, individual morale plummets.

In an educational setting communication is imperative and cannot be taken lightly. The conversations in this setting should be carefully planned and thoroughly thought out before any message is delivered. Educators have many different teaching styles, so when educating others, they must be very selective when communicating. Children and adults cannot be taught using the same style. Communication comes in many forms such as; writing, music, electronics, tone, verbal and non-verbal cues and all of them must be articulated with care according to the students age, demographics, and mental capabilities. In education, what an educator says is equally impactful as what they may fail to say when they are not prepared.

It is imperative that one must set the tone for the environment and take the initiative to create a pleasant rapport between administrators and staff members. Employees that are confident in their leader's ability to communicate precisely will help galvanize their peers and act as a bridge between management and subordinates. Many times, false assumptions occur because not enough information was given to complete a task. Therefore, supervisors and staff have to push the communication channel beyond the comfort zone making a path for solidarity and productivity.

Lack of Communication Barriers

1. **Closed channels of communication**. Some atmospheres discourage open discussion by the way they are set up or designed. The communication functions do not facilitate or encourage the free flow of dialogue between superiors and subordinates or peer to peer.

2. **Pseudo Open Door Policy**. Companies have open-door policies in words only; the door is closed. Superiors are ill-equipped to handle staff issues, and training is little to none.

3. **Information Desert** causes employee uncertainty, chaos, ambiguity, and insecurity.

4. **Climate Control.** A stiff communication climate stifles the free flow of clarifying information.

5. **Ineffective Leadership.** The leader does not take command of the communication process within the organization; thus, others try to fill the vacuum.

6. **Distractions.** Lack of communication occurs when leadership is distracted from the mission and goals of the company. Insignificant and irrelevant conversations cloud pertinent information, resulting in distractions, detours, and delays.

7. **Secrecy.** Organizations that hide essential information from their stakeholders open the door to lack of communication barriers and their consequences.

8. **Suppression.** Some leaders prohibit the sharing of information that does not agree with their personal viewpoint,

even though the information is relevant and will facilitate effective communication and positive outcomes.

9. **Stalling.** Sometimes information is stalled or held up awaiting the approval of the hierarchy to be released.

10. **Oppression.** Burdensome leadership withholds information until they are ready to share, even though it is crucial to the immediate success of the entire group.

Communication Strategies

1. Keep the lines of communication open. If you have a stated open-door policy, respect it and welcome those individuals in who decides to walk through the door. Be welcoming.
2. Learn active listening. Listen without interrupting and stay focus, refuse to allow your mind to wander, and focus on the conversation at hand.
3. Practice empathetic listening and communication, seek to understand first.
4. Become an assertive leader and communicator. Acknowledge that your staff can handle information adequately, it creates respect and trust.
5. Schedule regular meeting times to accommodate the consistent flow of communication, to keep staff in the loop.
6. Stay focused on the mission of the company and prioritizes your decisions based on the mission. Stay away from distracting communication and freely share and restate the company's mission often.
7. Open communication creates open doors. Opportunities are uncovered when communication announces the intention to move forward.
8. Freely share relevant information with all stakeholders.
9. Quickly release emails, memos, messages, directives, and any other communication that is important and beneficial to the company.
10. Don't put unnecessary burdens on the receiver of your

message, because you failed to take the time to use effective communication.

Notes

Chapter 5
No Communication

What happens when the communication completely stops? What is one's response to unanswered emails, texts, or phone calls? Messages that are not returned send an answer to a would-be receiver whether the missing in action sender meant it or not. What happens when you are expected to perform a specific task, you ask for clarification, and you get no response at all? Although poor communication is frustrating in the workplace, home, church, or any other situation, no response intensifies the anxiety and other negative emotions. Imagine standing in front of a brick wall asking for clarity concerning a previous communication and not getting any feedback whatsoever. How does the silence make you feel? Having the ability to effectively communicate with co-workers, subordinates, loved ones, and friends is an asset that not all people have. It is an unfortunate truth that there is the gatekeeper to an organization that are sometimes tasked with stifling all incoming communication. Gatekeepers are charged with the task to manage the flow of information coming in and going out, and at times the gatekeeper is overzealous resulting in an array of communication mess. Therefore, it is true; without a vision, failure is assured, and, without substantial communication collapse is imminent.

No communication is the result of a total breakdown of communication between one or more parties. Usually, there is an underlying emotion or event that precipitated an entire shutdown of conversation. When communication dries up, it creates chaos and confusion among workers, family members, partners, friends, etc. It is very difficult to overcome although not impossible. Organizations have communication structures that are formal and informal, either way, there is a method, a way that information is shared from department to department or person to person, to ensure continuity and cohesiveness remains. Subsequently, when the information channels dry up, tension mounts and misunderstanding grips the people who are caught up in the veil of silence. Unfortunately, unintended consequences develop when communication shuts down that severely cripple an operation. One such result is misunderstanding and mistakes. Instructions or information that are not adequately given or not spoken at all leads to frustration, misunderstandings, wasted time, and possibly lost marriage or relationship due to NO communications. Depending on the type of communication needed it could be fatal.

When communication breaks down, there are immediate areas to investigate to uncover the reasons why, with the intent to reestablish conversation and move forward. Every organization has a culture and personality, mostly established by the leader. The leader determines the communication model for the others to follow. If the leader is free-flowing with information, the company usually is ripe with information and conversation; conversely, if the leadership is stingy with the flow of information, the group is information-starved, and the vision suffers.

There is not a choice of whether communication must take place, it must happen. It is true; there are some instances where communication is not needed maybe as much than others, but, there is no place for the absence of communication, it is the life line of every situation in this world.

Remember, the form and the content of communication is specific to each individual and group. There are cultures where communication is like breathing air, it happens without thinking about it. And, there are cultures where communication is not as rich and naturally flowing.

Some people share information on a need to know basis. As mentioned earlier in this book, leadership plays a major factor in the process. When the information flow becomes a one-way, everyone involved suffers. The danger of No communication is everything is functioning falsely, and if there is no responsibility then there is no accountability, and everyone loses.

No Communication Barriers

1. **Conversation Breakdown.** The conversation completely stops between two or more individuals. Indeed, organization conversational communication breakdown, is a symptom of a deep fissure.

2. **Culture Shock**. The feeling of disorientation and bewilderment experienced by a person who is suddenly exposed to a new or strange environment.

3. **Personality Traits.** Some personalities are prone to silent communication, they are extreme introverts and share only what they deem crucial.

4. **Controlling Communicator.** A controlling communicator keeps a tight lid on the communication flow, allowing only what he or she wants to be distributed.

5. **Lack of Interest.** Some people have little interest in participating in the flow of communication. They choose to remain silent until the time arises when they are forced to share.

6. **Misunderstood Roles.** The roles in an organization are not well defined, causing some communication to go missing.

7. **Buried Emotions.** Some people choose to not voice their discontent, but rather they use silence to express their dissatisfaction.

8. **Lack of Communication Competencies.** Some people are inept communicators.

9. **Confused Messaging**. Some organizations have competing messages, causing some individuals to go silent.

10. **No Communication.** Simply having no interest in the situation whatsoever.

Calming Communication Barriers

1. **Break the silence.** For the good of the organization, restart the conversation and complete the tasks or projects.

2. **Research the culture of the company, and its workers.** Learn to adapt and function within the unique environments. People will talk with those they trust.

3. **Take time to understand the differences.** Don't seek to change others, rather accept a person for who they are. There is uniqueness in everyone embrace it.

4. **Controlled Confrontation**. Sometimes it is crucial to have information now, therefore learn to confront without the heat of a confrontation. Tact is key.

5. **Make your conversation as engaging as possible.** When people appear disinterested, turn up the engagement and talk about something that peaks their interest.

6. **Find something interesting in another person's interpersonal communication style.** Speak to the person not the situation.

7. **Understand your role and the roles of others.** Know your lane and ride in it to perfection. Don't cross into another person's lane.

8. **Don't Suffer in Silence.** Don't stew; speak up! If something is bothering you let it be known you have the right to be heard.

9. **Study the art of Communication.** Study, learn, practice, and repeat.

10. **Get The Message Right.** Before you share the information make sure it is correct. Mixed messages create Communication Barriers.

Notes

Conclusion
Genre: Personal Growth & Development

There has been a lot of time, energy, research, and perhaps even some misunderstandings along the way during the writing process of "Calming Communication Barriers" Yet, through it all it has been a great learning process for myself, my family, my friends and Publisher, Dr. Laura Brown. We have tried to make sure each area of communication was targeted and met through a variety of literature, examples, expressions, and through sharing a few clichés to help empower you with the necessary tools and strategies you can use when you need them!

Our goal was to keep this book as informative, intellectual, down to earth, and in a few spaces even humorous to help assist you at a time when you need reiteration in your communication! "Think of it as a handy tool" We all have experienced times when our communication was not as effective or even appropriate for certain situations. There were times when we didn't know what to say or perhaps how to say it, but now you do not have to experience those issues any more. The strategies are tailored for the use in your business, professional, and personal life as well! You have tools to remind you what not to say but you also have alternative tools to help teach you what to say.

So, it is with my deepest sincere regards and prayers that everyone that purchases this book finds the tools, strategies, and examples very easy to apply to your day to day lives! I hope that you can stop and think about not only what you are going to say when you are communicating with others but how what you say will affect them. The way you convey a message determines how the message will be perceived. So please as you prepare to communicate with others be kind, selective in your tone, volume, body language and your method of deliverance, because it all plays a part in how your message is perceived!

A special thanks to my publisher DR. Laura Brown, I know there were times when you thought I could not have been using the strategies that I was teaching on right☺ Just want you to know that I was!!! And that I love you and I appreciate all that you have done to make this collaborative piece a success. No! it was not easy, but we did it against all odds!

I also will like to give Homage and honor to my Pastor & FirstLady Apostle Edward & Mattie Jackson and my Christ Kingdom Ministries Family!

My Mentor, Mother in the Ministry, & friend: Rev, Willie Mae Harvey

I salute my family, my children, and my grandchildren for putting up with me and my working & homework tantrums for the last 13 years!!! Thank u, Thank u, Thank u, too the Lover of my life Jesus Christ of Nazareth!!!

Communication By The Numbers

1. Communication Barriers: 26,041 is the cumulative cost per worker per year due to productivity losses resulting from communication barriers.

2. A Gallup poll says 70% of U.S. employees are not engaged. Actively disengaged employees cost the U.S. $450 to 550 billion per year in lost productivity.

3. When employees understand their overall role in business 91% will work towards that success.

4. Companies that have highly effective communication have 47% higher return to shareholders.

5. Return of investment are impacts of poor internal communication barriers, retention, performance, internal communication profits, and employee engagement.

6. 70% of companies say that retaining talent is their top priority and challenge.

7. 71% of employees feel leaders do not spend enough time explaining goals and plans.

8. The least engaged workers are also less committed and are more likely to leave the organization sooner.

9. Workers with higher levels of commitment are 87% less likely to leave an organization.

10. Better companies exist because of better communication.

Takeaways

1. Effective communication influences an organization's success or failure.

2. Effective communication skill is the most sought characteristic of hiring professionals.

3. An organization that has leaders with great communication skills enjoys better retention rates.

4. There are quantifiable barriers that cause effective communication break downs.

5. Negative productivity in the workplace has a direct correlation to ineffective communication.

6. Billions of dollars are lost annually due to poor communication.

7. When groups join forces on one accord to make effective communication a priority, every aspect of the group will improve.

8. Unnecessary breaks occur in relationships because of miscommunication, mistrust, and misunderstanding.

9. Clarity and conciseness will clear up many communication issues.

10. Always seek to understand the other person first.

Change a Communication Barrier Habit In 7 Days

Instructions:

1. Choose one of the communication barriers that adversely affect your communication outcomes.

2. Choose one strategy to apply to the barrier for 7 consecutive days.

3. WRITE down your attempts, challenges, and victories each day; Big or Small, they ALL count!

4. TIP: Choose a barrier that will make a significant impact on your communication style such as: interrupting or not clarifying.

5. Track your emotions everyday during the 7 days you are confronting your barriers.

6. Note any changes in your attitude as well as the changes in attitude of those you engage.

7. Commit to endure the entire 7 days.

DAY 1

Communication Barrier:

Strategy:

Outcome:

DAY 2

Communication Barrier:

Strategy:

Outcome:

DAY 3

Communication Barrier:

Strategy:

Outcome:

DAY 4

Communication Barrier:

Strategy:

Outcome:

DAY 5

Communication Barrier:

Strategy:

Outcome:

DAY 6

Communication Barrier:

Strategy:

Outcome:

DAY 7

Communication Barrier:

Strategy:

Outcome: